FAND♥M FEVER

TAYLOR SWIFT'S
SWIFTIES

BY VIRGINIA LOH-HAGAN

45TH PARALLEL PRESS

Published in the United States of America by
Cherry Lake Publishing Group
Ann Arbor, Michigan
www.cherrylakepublishing.com

Reading Adviser: Beth Walker Gambro, MS, Ed., Reading Consultant, Yorkville, IL
Content Advisers: Carrlee Craig and Shelby Jenkins
Book Designer: Joseph Hatch

45th Parallel Press is an imprint of Cherry Lake Publishing Group.

Library of Congress Cataloging-in-Publication Data

Names: Loh-Hagan, Virginia, author.
Title: Taylor Swift's Swifties / Virginia Loh-Hagan.
Description: Ann Arbor : 45th Parallel Press, 2024. | Series: Fandom fever | Audience:
   Grades 4-6 | Summary: "Taylor Swift's Swifties provides an inside look at the powerful
   fandom of Taylor Swift. Readers will get hooked on this hi-lo title, covering facts
   about and insights into the group of fans who aren't afraid to make their support of
   Tay Swift known"— Provided by publisher.
Identifiers: LCCN 2024009456 | ISBN 9781668947487 (hardcover) | ISBN 9781668948873
   (paperback) | ISBN 9781668950395 (ebook) | ISBN 9781668954959 (pdf)
Subjects: LCSH: Swift, Taylor, 1989—Juvenile literature. | Popular music fans—Juvenile
   literature.
Classification: LCC ML3930.S989 L65 2024 | DDC 782.42164092—dc23/eng/20240227
LC record available at https://lccn.loc.gov/2024009456

Cherry Lake Publishing Group would like to acknowledge the work of the Partnership for
21st Century Learning, a Network of Battelle for Kids. Please visit Battelle for Kids online
for more information.

Note from publisher: Websites change regularly, and their future contents are outside
of our control. Supervise children when conducting any recommended online searches
for extended learning opportunities.

Printed in the United States of America

Table of Contents

Dr. Virginia Loh-Hagan is an author and educator. She is currently the Director of the Asian Pacific Islander Desi American (APIDA) Center at San Diego State University and the Co-Executive Director of The Asian American Education Project. She lives in San Diego with her very tall husband and very naughty dogs.

Fandoms can be about anything. They can be about singers, TV shows, video games, books, and more.

CHAPTER ONE

From Fan Base to Fandom

Musicians make music. They perform music. Some become big stars. They become **celebrities**. Celebrities are famous. They have a **fan base**. A fan base is a group of supporters.

Most fans have a casual interest. But some fans are more devoted. They worship their **idols**. Idols are big stars. Devoted fans form **fandoms**. Fandoms are communities. They're networks of fans.

Fandoms of musicians are special groups. They buy the musicians' music. They buy their **merch**. Merch means merchandise. It means stuff that can be sold. Merch includes shirts and posters. Fans follow musicians on tour. They attend their shows. They go on tour with them. They connect with the music. They connect with the messages. They sing their songs. They know all the words.

Fandoms are a powerful force. They can influence music. They use the internet. The internet gives fans information about their idols. It gives them more access to their idols. It also gives them more access to other fans.

Fans build relationships with each other. They share their knowledge. They share their passion. They build connections. They create content. They share content.

Fans make fan art. This is when they draw pictures of their idols. Fans also write stories about their idols. This is called fan fiction. They share their art. They share their stories.

Some celebrities have large fandoms. Their fandoms even have special names. That's a sign of success!

Some fandoms are referred to as "manias." An example is "Beatlemania." This was when fans first started loving The Beatles.

Taylor Swift won her first Grammys in 2010. She won "Best Country Album," "Best Country Song," "Best Female Country Vocal Performance," and "Album of the Year" for *Fearless*.

CHAPTER TWO

Fanning Taylor Swift

Taylor Swift was born in 1989. She's a big star. She's an American singer. She's also a songwriter. She started at a young age. By age 10, she was singing at local events. By age 12, she was writing her own songs. At age 14, she had a record contract.

Swift started by singing country songs. Now she sings pop songs. Her songs are top hits. She performs all around the world. Her shows sell out. She always has big crowds. She has sold many albums. She has won many awards. She just won TIME's "Person of the Year" award. She just won her fourth "Album of the Year" Grammy. She has lots of fans. Her fandom is known as the Swifties.

Swift was one of the first pop stars to use social media. She did this in 2005. This started her fan base. "Love Story" and "You Belong with Me" became hits. She gained more fans.

Swifties first emerged around 2010. They're one of the largest fandoms. In 2012, Swift had an interview. She said she thought the name was adorable. In 2017, she **trademarked** it. Trademark means to own the brand.

Swifties feel like they grew up with Taylor. Swift shares her personal life. Swifties can relate to her. They say her **lyrics** feel like their diaries. Lyrics are the words of songs.

Taylor Swift writes about her love life. "We Are Never Ever Getting Back Together" was her first song to hit number 1 on the Billboard Hot 100 Chart. It was from the *Red* album.

SUPER FAN

Derek Hennen is a Swiftie. But he's also a scientist. For years, he and his team collected millipedes. They traveled to 17 states. Hennen played Swift's music in the car. He was in Tennessee. He was at Fall Creek Falls State Park. He discovered a new type of millipede. This happened in 2022. Millipedes have long bodies. They have many legs. The legs reminded Hennen of Swift. Also, Swift moved to Tennessee to start her career. This is another reason why Hennen thought of Swift. The millipede was named the Swift twisted-claw millipede. Its scientific name is Nannaria swiftae. Hennen said Swift's music has "gotten him through 'some rough times'." He listens to Swift while working. His favorite songs are "New Romantics" and "betty." He said, "What better way to thank her for the joy that her music has brought me then to name a little species of millipede after her."

A newspaper said Swift and Swifties are "all part of one big friend group." Swift engages her fans. She sends them messages. She sends them clues. She does this in her songs. She does this in her social media posts. She does this in her interviews. Swifties like to **decode** them. Decode means to figure out.

Swift connects with her fans. She gives them gifts. She invites them to attend special events. She's made surprise visits. She attends their events. She gives away free tickets. She's paid off bills. She even bought a house for a fan in need.

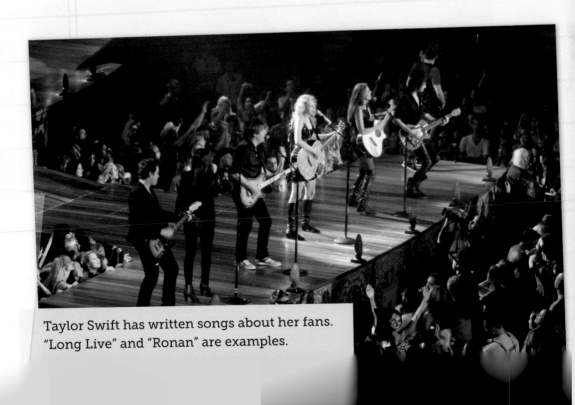

Taylor Swift has written songs about her fans. "Long Live" and "Ronan" are examples.

Swifties make themed bracelets. They give them out to other fans. They also trade them.

CHAPTER THREE

Living That Fan Life

Swifties show up at Taylor Swift events. To be a Swiftie, make sure to look the part! Do the following:

+ Wear fun outfits. Outfits should sparkle. Wear glitter. Wear sequins. Wear bright or **pastel** colors. Pastels are soft, pale colors.

+ Wear cowboy boots. Swift's roots are in country music. Cowboy boots represent country music.

+ Wear several friendship bracelets. Stack them on your arms. These bracelets can be made from threads. They can be made with beads.

+ Paint or draw the number 13 on your hands. This is Swift's favorite number. Swift was born on December 13. She turned 13 on Friday the 13th. Her first album went gold in 13 weeks. Her first #1 song had a 13-second introduction.

Swifties have their own culture. To be a Swiftie, make sure to act the part! Do the following:

+ Analyze Swift's words. Swifties are part of "Swiftology." They work together. They post to online discussions. They look for hidden messages. They interpret meanings.

+ Host or attend Swift-themed parties. "Swiftogeddon" is an example. It's when clubs host Swift-themed events. Fans dance and sing to Swift songs. They hang with other fans.

+ Respect Swift's "eras." Swift likes to try different types of music. Each era is a different style or mood. Swift changes her image. She changes her sound. This increases her fans. Swifties stick with her.

"All Too Well" mentions a scarf. It is a very deep, emotional song. Fans feel connected to it. The scarf is a big topic for Swifties.

Fanatic Fan

On May 20, 2022, Taylor Swift performed at Gillette Stadium. The stadium is outside of Boston, Massachusetts. More than 200,000 fans attended over the course of 3 shows there. Swift performed for about 3.5 hours. She performed in the pouring rain. A Swiftie got an idea. But they may have gone too far. This fan tried to sell the rainwater. They filled small containers. They priced each container at $250. The containers were labeled "Taylor Swift Eras Tour Merch Rain." Some fans thought it was funny. Some fans did not. The containers may have been a joke. But no one really knows. The posting has been taken down. There were other postings. Fans sold bracelets they wore at the show. These bracelets cost $10. Other fans were selling confetti from the show. The confetti cost $15. Confetti is bits of paper. It's thrown at the end of Swift's shows.

Not all fan behavior is good. Some fans can be **toxic**. Toxic means harmful. To be a Swiftie, don't let your passion become poison. Do the following:

+ Respect Swift's privacy. Toxic fans have stalked her. They find her. They swarm her. For example, Swift attended her friend's wedding. Toxic fans showed up. They chanted Swift's name. They ruined this event.

+ Avoid interfering in Swift's life. Swifties follow Swift's love life. Toxic fans have sent threats to her ex-boyfriends. They harass anyone who's mean to Swift.

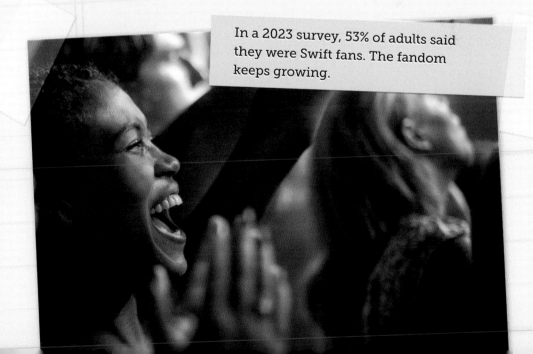

In a 2023 survey, 53% of adults said they were Swift fans. The fandom keeps growing.

CHAPTER FOUR

The Power of Fandom

Swifties are inspired by their idol. They support her. They support her causes. Together, they're a powerful force. They've helped people. They've made social changes.

Swifties help other Swifties. In 2023, a fan went to one of Swift's shows. He was heading home. He was killed by a drunk driver. Thousands of fans donated money. Many donated $13. They did this to honor Swift's favorite number. They raised more than $125,000 for the fan's family.

Swifties have passed laws. In 2023, millions of fans tried to buy tickets for her Eras tour. **Bots** are computer programs. They bought many tickets. They did this before fans could buy them. This raised prices. Swifties thought this was unfair. They wanted to ban bots. Texas passed a "Save our Swifties" law.

Taylor Swift has a record for highest ticket sales in 1 day. More than 2.4 million tickets were sold the first day on sale for her Eras tour.

Swifties protect rights. From 2014 to 2015, Swift fought for artists to be paid more. She fought against music streaming services. Streaming offers content online. The companies refused to pay artists more. So Swift didn't use the streaming services. Instead, she released her new albums on **CD** and **vinyl**. CD is a compact disc. It stores music. Vinyl refers to record albums. Both CD and vinyl formats became outdated. Streaming took over. Companies doubted Swift could sell her music. But Swifties proved them wrong. Fans bought her CDs. They bought her records. In this way, Swifties start trends. In the 2020s, Swifties helped revive vinyl records.

"The Taylor Swift effect" is real. Swifties attend concerts. This increases money for cities.

Idol Inspiration

Idols have idols! Taylor Swift is inspired by Shania Twain. Twain is known as the "Queen of Country Pop." Swift and Twain have a lot in common. They're both singers and songwriters. They both crossed over from country to pop. They both sold millions of records. They both put on high-energy shows. They're both big stars. In some ways, Twain paved the way for Swift. She made country pop popular. Swift listened to Twain. She said Twain inspired her to pursue country music. She said Twain's music made her "want to just run around the block four times and daydream about everything." She wore a shirt with Twain on it. Twain said it was "really cool" to see her wearing it. She said, "Isn't she a doll?... I feel like I'm her aunt or something...We're in sync in a lot of ways."

CHAPTER FIVE

Insider Information

Fans know their idols. They can also spot fake fans. Make sure you do your research. Here are the top 10 things every true Swiftie should know about Taylor Swift!

1. Swift grew up in Pennsylvania. Her family had a Christmas tree farm. This inspired a Christmas song. She wrote it in 2019. The song is called "Christmas Tree Farm."

2. Swift was named after well-known musician James Taylor. Swift loved music from an early age. At age 3, she'd walk up to strangers. She'd sing songs from *The Lion King*.

3. Swift was given her first album at age 6. The record was *Blue* by LeAnn Rimes.

Taylor Swift's family moved to Nashville, Tennessee. They did this to support her. Nashville is the capital of country music.

Taylor Swift is a big reader. Books have inspired many of her songs. She has supported libraries.

4. Swift was bullied in school. Bullies teased her for being awkward. They teased her for being annoying. They teased her for being tall. Writing songs was healing for her.

5. Swift learned to play the guitar at age 12. A computer repairman taught her. He showed her how to play three chords. Then she wrote her first song. The song was called "Lucky You."

6. Swift wrote a book. She was 14 years old. Her book was 350 pages. It was called A Girl Named Girl. It's about a mother who wants a son but has a daughter. Her parents have the only copy.

7. Swift's first single was "Tim McGraw." This song is about a boyfriend who moved away. It became a hit. It launched her career.

8. Swift loves cats. Her cats are named after movie and TV characters. They include Olivia Benson, Meredith Grey, and Benjamin Button. Swift also acted in the musical movie Cats.

9. Swift puts her heart into all her songs. "Wildest Dreams" is special. She recorded her own heartbeat. Other songs feature real sounds.

10. Swift has many awards. She has broken more than 50 Guinness World Records. She's the first female artist on Spotify with 100 million monthly listeners. She has the most American Music Awards. She has the most streamed album in 24 hours.

There's so much more to learn! Make sure to keep up with the latest.

Taylor Swift funded the Taylor Swift Education Center. This center is at the Country Music Hall of Fame. The museum is in Nashville.

Fans have their own language. Here are some Swiftie words you should know:

+ **Blondie:** Blondie is a nickname for Swift.

+ **From the Vault:** "The vault" refers to songs that didn't make it onto an album.

+ **Secret Sessions:** Swift has hosted special events for her fans. These "Secret Sessions" were listening parties. Swift hosted these before her album releases. She hosted them at her house.

+ **Senior Swifties:** These fans usually belong to the Baby Boomer (1946–1964) and Generation X (1965–1980) generations.

+ **Swiftmas:** Swifties celebrate Swift's birthday. Swiftmas is held on December 13. Swift is known to send early Christmas gifts to fans.

+ **SwiftTok:** SwiftTok is a community on TikTok. Swifties share content there.

+ **Taylor's Version:** Taylor's Version refers to Swift's rereleased songs.

+ **Taylurking:** This term refers to Swift spying on her fans online. Swift said, "I cyber-stalk because I care."

+ **TayTay:** TayTay is a nickname for Swift. Swifties add "Tay" to words. An example is saying "TayTastic" instead of "fantastic."

Taylor Swift said, "...Fans are my favorite thing in the world. I've never been the type of artist who has that line drawn between their friends and their fans. The line's always been really blurred for me. I'll hang out with them after the show. I'll hang out with them before the show. If I see them in the mall, I'll stand there and talk to them for 10 minutes."

There are all types of Swifties. Swifties are all around the world. Start your own fan club!

+ Promote your fan club.

+ Host a meeting.

+ Collect a list of names.

+ Have fun!

+ Plan events.

Taylor Swift has been called "America's most important musician."

GLOSSARY

bots (BAHTZ) software applications programmed to do certain tasks

celebrities (suh-LEH-bruh-teez) well-known or famous people

CD (SEE DEE) short for compact disc, a flat plastic disk used to store recorded music

decode (dee-KOHD) figure out a puzzle or mystery

fan base (FAN BAYSS) group of fans for a particular sport, musical group, or celebrity

fandom (FAN-duhm) subculture, community, or network of fans who share a common interest

idols (EYE-duhlz) people who are greatly admired and loved by others

lyrics (LEER-iks) words to songs

merch (MURCH) short for merchandise, which includes posters, shirts, and other items

pastels (pa-STELZ) soft, pale colors

toxic (TAHK-sik) harmful

trademark (TRAYD-mark) word, phrase, or symbol legally registered as representing a company or product

vinyl (VY-nuhl) large vinyl disk that stores recorded music

LEARN MORE

Anderson, Kirsten. *Who is Taylor Swift?* New York, NY: Penguin Workshop, 2024.

Krull, Kathleen, and Virginia Loh-Hagan. *Born Reading: 20 Stories of Women Reading Their Way Into History.* New York, NY: Simon & Schuster/Paula Wiseman Books, 2023.

Layton, Kitty. *Be More Taylor: Fearless Advice on Following Your Dreams and Finding Your Voice.* New York, NY: DK Publishing, 2022.

INDEX